CONTENTS

D1293883

PICTURE AN ANIMAL

If you were going to draw an animal, what would it be?
You have so much choice, it might be hard to decide! Animals are
a great subject for artists because there are so many shapes, colors,
and characters to choose from. Friendly pets, fierce wild beasts,
bright birds, and even imaginary creatures have made their
way into paintings, sculptures, and other works of art.

Look at the different ways in which **animals have inspired
famous artists**—and then **let them inspire you, too!** Each
page of this book will tell you about a work of art and the person
who created it. When you lift the flap, you'll find a project based
on the artwork. Don't feel you have to copy it exactly.
Half the fun of art is making something your own!

GETTING STARTED

There's a checklist on page 31 that will tell you
what you need for each project, but it's a good idea
to read through the steps before you begin. There
are also some handy tips on the next page . . .

Always have a **pencil** and
eraser handy. Making a
rough **sketch** can help you
plan a project and see how
it's going to look.

PICK YOUR PAINT . . .

Acrylic paints are thick and bright—they're great for strong colors and for textures such as shaggy fur. **Poster paints** are cheaper than acrylics but still bright. Use them when you need a lot of paint.

Watercolors give a thinner coloring—try them over oil pastel or crayon, or draw over them in ink.

Use a mixture of thick and thin **paintbrushes**. Have a glass jar or plastic cup of water ready to rinse them in and a **palette** or paper plate for mixing paint.

acrylic paint

Lay some newspaper on your surface before you start to paint!

watercolor paint

sponged paint

TRY PASTELS . . .

Oil pastels have a bright, waxy look, like crayons. **Soft pastels** can be smudged and blended like chalk.

For painting, use thick **drawing** or **watercolor paper**—anything too thin will wrinkle. **Pastel paper** has a rough surface that holds on to the color.

Collect a range of **colored paper and card stock** for collages and 3-D models.

oil pastels

soft pastel

Ready to start?
Let's **get into art!**

Look around the home for other art materials. Useful things include sponges, rags or cloths, toothpicks, drinking straws, scissors, glue, string, roller brushes, and a hole punch.

In real life, this picture is enormous
—almost 10 feet (3 meters) square!
It's a collage of painted paper
stuck onto white paper and then
onto canvas. Matisse called this
method "drawing with scissors."

THE SNAIL

Henri Matisse 1953

You might have to look twice before spotting the snail in this picture! There's no outline, but Henri Matisse has created the idea of a snail by arranging colored shapes in a spiral pattern.

Drawing with color

When Matisse made *The Snail*, he was 84 years old. He wasn't well enough to stand and draw, so instead he used color as his starting point. His assistants painted sheets of paper in plain colors, and then Matisse cut or tore them into shapes.

Matisse chose his colors carefully. They are not the colors of a real snail, but they are warm and bright. Matisse knew that complementary colors, such as red and green, look stronger when they're put next to each other. The way he has placed the pieces makes them zing out, as if the snail is moving. It seems to be wriggling out of the jagged orange frame!

WHO WAS MATISSE?

Henri Matisse was born in France in 1869. His first job was as a lawyer, but he didn't like it much. At the age of 20, he became ill and had to spend long hours in bed. His mother gave him a paint box to pass the time, and right away he knew he would become an artist! Matisse made many famous paintings in his distinctive, colorful style.

Let some pieces overlap the border.

3 Lay the shapes in a twisting pattern, thinking about which colors you are placing next to one another.

4 Move the shapes around until you're happy with your snake, and then glue them down.

Use a big piece for the head. If you like, you can add a forked tongue!

SNIP A SNAKE

Matisse loved finding patterns in nature. Look at some pictures of snakes to see how they bend and curl, and then try making this snaky collage.

Your sheet can be huge, like Matisse's, or small if you have less space.

straight edge here

1 Take a white sheet of card stock or posterboard as your base. Cut out some strips of colored paper—use the edges of the paper so they're straight along one side. Lay them around your card stock to make a border. Glue them down.

2 To make your snake, cut out simple block shapes from different colored pieces of paper.

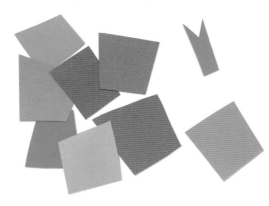

SUSPENSE

Sir Edwin Landseer 1861

Who is this dog waiting for? What's behind the door?
Landseer wanted us to ask questions like this when he painted *Suspense*! His picture tells a story, but he leaves us to figure out what it is.

See the story
If you look closely, you'll spot some clues. There are drops of blood on the floor . . . a feather torn from a hat . . . a knight's armored gloves on the table. It seems that the dog's master has been wounded and carried through the house.

The dog sits on his haunches, staring closely at the door. We can tell that he is worried and longs to rush to his master's side. Landseer's skillful brushwork makes us feel that the animal is alive. The light glints on his anxious face, and hairs stand up on his neck. He leans forward, ready to spring up at any moment—but we can only imagine what he'll find.

WHO WAS LANDSEER?

Sir Edwin Landseer was born into a family of artists in England in 1802. He began to draw as soon as he could hold a pencil and was exhibiting work by the age of 13. Animals were his favorite subjects—he even had a breed of dog named after him! Landseer made sculptures, too, including four huge bronze lions in London's Trafalgar Square.

Vary the length of the streaks.

3 Now paint white highlights using short flicks of a fine brush. Use dark paint for the eye, nose, and mouth, and a few shadowy streaks under the belly.

Here are some other ways of **painting fur**.

Dab dark then light paint with a piece of sponge.

FURRY FRIENDS

Landseer's work was very detailed, but **you can paint furry animals in different ways.** Try these!

Use the brush tip for the tail, legs, and ears.

1 Use a square-ended brush to paint the basic shape—it could be a dog like this, or your own pet or other favorite animal.

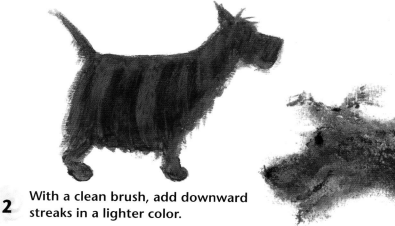

2 With a clean brush, add downward streaks in a lighter color.

Scratch into thick, wet paint with a toothpick.

CRINKLY GIRAFFE

Alexander Calder 1971

This giraffe isn't going anywhere— but if you walk around it, it almost seems to move. Calder was famous for his dynamic sculptures, some of which really do move.

Animobiles

Crinkly Giraffe is made of painted metal cut into simple shapes. The flat metal looks different from different angles, so the crinkly neck seems to shift and turn. Calder made a whole series of crinkly animals like this. His wife named them animobiles!

The word *animobile* comes from *animal* and *mobile*—and Calder invented the mobile, too. His first one had a motor, but he soon realized that hanging shapes would move on their own. He experimented with different materials, including metal, wire, and wood. Little did he know how popular his invention would become!

WHO WAS CALDER?

Alexander Calder was born in 1898 in the United States. His father was a sculptor and his mother a painter, but Alexander studied to be an engineer. Later, he went to art school and traveled to Paris, France, to work. He used nature as his inspiration for abstract mobiles, standing "stabiles," and giant outdoor sculptures that are displayed around the world.

Stick the
head on
here.

3 Glue one end of the neck to the body and then stick on the head. Next glue on the arms, followed by the legs and tail.

4 Dangle your monkey from a hook, shelf, or doorknob. Then make some monkey friends!

Try hanging one monkey from another!

CRINKLY MONKEYS

Calder turned flat materials into 3-D objects. Try it yourself with these crinkly monkeys!

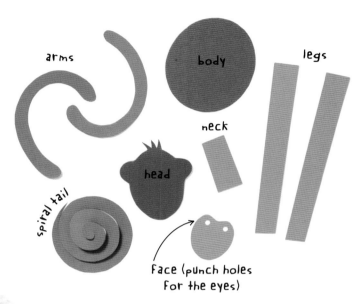

arms

body

legs

neck

head

spiral tail

face (punch holes for the eyes)

1 Cut out shapes like these from colored card stock.

In 1926, Calder made a whole circus of animals and actors out of wood, wire, cork, and cloth. He kept them in suitcases and traveled around giving performances!

legs

spiral tail

neck

2 Fold the leg and neck strips back and forth to make them crinkly. Gently stretch out the tail. Glue the face onto the head.

THE BIRD

Georges Braque 1949

On first glance, you might think a child made this picture! The shapes are simple and the colors are bright. In fact, Braque created it for children, as part of a project for schools in the United Kingdom after World War II.

Primary print

The idea came from a woman in London, England who decided that schools should have great pieces of art on their walls. She traveled to Paris, France, and persuaded artists such as Braque to help. They produced work using a new type of lithograph printing. Each print had a border around the edge, so there wasn't any need for a frame!

Braque was fond of bold, simple shapes—and he particularly loved painting birds. In this print, the shapes are familiar, but they float in an imaginary scene. The primary colors red, yellow, and blue look cheerful and fresh against the white.

WHO WAS BRAQUE?

Georges Braque was born in France in 1882. He trained as a painter and decorator but studied art in the evenings and soon took up Fauvism—a new style of painting in bright colors. He then turned to Cubism, using simple shapes and collage. During World War I, he was injured and had to stop painting. Later, he experimented with prints and sculpture.

2 Taking one shape at a time, cover the outline with strong craft glue. Stick a piece of thick string or cord all around it.

Try gluing on some other materials. They need to be as thick as the string.

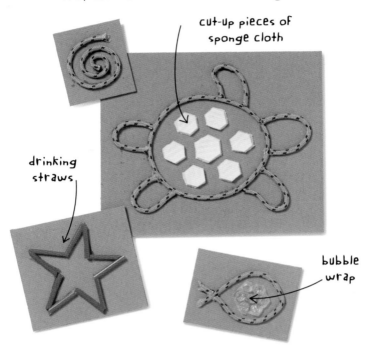

cut-up pieces of sponge cloth

drinking straws

bubble wrap

4 Cut out your best prints and glue them onto colored paper.

Dip the end of a straw or pencil in white paint to print some bubbles!

Use simple shapes like Braque's to make a

SEASIDE STRING PRINT

1 First draw your seaside shapes onto thick cardboard.

Choose one main animal and some smaller shapes.

3 When the glue is dry, use a roller or sponge to spread paint over the design. Turn it over onto a piece of white paper. Press firmly, and then gently lift it off.

The print will be in reverse.

If you don't get a good print the first time, try again!

PEACOCK AND MAGPIE

Edward Bawden 1970

What's the first thing you notice in this picture? Probably the peacock with its dazzling, fanned-out tail! Bawden shows us the proud character of the bird in this illustration of one of Aesop's Fables.

A telling tail

Fables are stories with a moral, which means they have a lesson to teach us. In this one, the peacock declares that he should be king of the birds. The others are impressed by his grand appearance, but the magpie questions whether he could protect the birds against eagles and other hunters. The moral is to listen to the advice of others.

Bawden cut this scene into linoleum and then printed it in ink on paper. The crisp lines make the story clear, but they are decorative, too. The yellow of the peacock catches our eye, just as it attracts the birds. Only when we look more closely do we see the magpie talking wisely to the crowd.

WHO WAS BAWDEN?

Edward Bawden was born in England in 1903. He became famous for many types of art, including book illustrations, advertising posters, murals, and metalwork furniture. He made tile paintings for the London Underground (the subway) and even designed china for passenger ships!

3 Now squeeze some dark blue and dark green acrylic paint onto a palette or paper plate. Paint over the oil pastel—try to work quickly and lay the paint on thickly.

Paint the green tail and then the blue spots and body.

You could use the end of a paintbrush...

a toothpick...

or the tip of a teaspoon.

Try scraping into paint to create some

FABULOUS FEATHERS

1 Draw the outline of a peacock on a piece of thick paper or card stock. Start with the body and then add a big, fanlike tail.

Draw circular markings on the tail.

2 Color your peacock with a thick layer of oil pastel. Use light, bright colors like these.

4 While the paint is still wet, scrape feathery patterns into it. If you make a mistake, just paint over it and scrape again!

The oil pastel colors show through.

FISH (E59)

M. C. Escher 1942

No matter how hard you look, you won't find a gap between these fish! Escher has taken the shape of an animal and turned it into a perfect pattern. It's called a tessellation.

Tile style

Tessellation is basically tiling— every shape fits together edge to edge. Of course, it's much harder to tile an animal shape than a simple square or triangle! Escher used geometric shapes as his starting point, then changed them into curving forms. He twisted, flipped, and repeated them to make patterns.

We can see two types of fish in this picture. It's like looking through a kaleidoscope. Escher drew them on graph paper and then colored them with pencils, ink, and watercolor. He liked the idea that the pattern could go on forever, though he had to stop when he got near the edge of the page!

WHO WAS ESCHER?

Maurits Cornelis Escher was born in the Netherlands in 1898. His interest in linking shapes began on a trip to the Alhambra, a Moorish castle in Spain. He drew and sketched on his travels and went home to make prints of the buildings he'd seen. In his work, he loved to trick the eye and play with impossible spaces. He turned the world into a puzzling and unbelievable place!

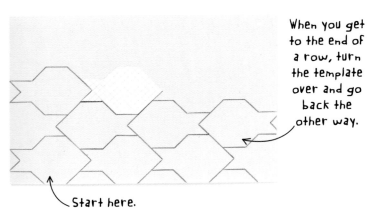

When you get to the end of a row, turn the template over and go back the other way.

Start here.

3 At the bottom of a large sheet of paper, draw around your template in pencil. Then move it along so that the tail slots into the head and draw around it again. Keep going like this!

These fish were outlined in marker, shaded with oil pastel, then washed over with watercolor paint.

Make this simple template for an Escher-style
FISH SQUISH

Escher made 137 drawings like this one. He created patterns using lizards, frogs, insects, birds, and even human shapes. His work has always fascinated mathematicians—but surprisingly, Escher struggled with math in school!

1 Glue a piece of graph paper to some card stock and cut out a 2 x 2 in. (5cm x 5cm) square. Mark two triangles across opposite corners, as shown.

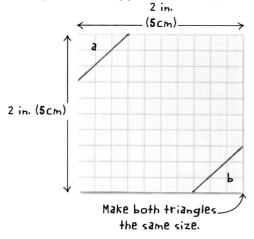

2 in.
(5cm)

2 in. (5cm)

a

b

Make both triangles the same size.

2 Cut off one triangle and carefully tape it to the other side of the square, like this.

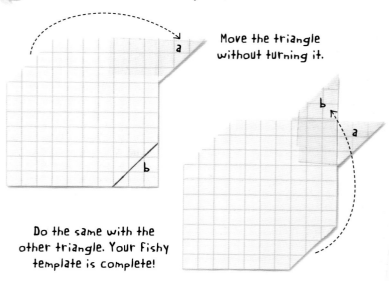

Move the triangle without turning it.

a

b

b

a

Do the same with the other triangle. Your fishy template is complete!

4 When you've got a full page of fish, color them in!

CARNIVAL OF HARLEQUIN

Joan Miró 1924–1925

Have you ever seen things in a dream that wouldn't make sense in real life? Miró takes us to a dreamlike place in this painting of a strange but lively party!

Carnival chaos

The creatures here aren't animals as we know them, but you can probably recognize some shapes. There are winged insects, spidery forms, a fish, and two cats playing with string. Bright characters leap across the canvas, dancing to musical notes that are floating in the air.

When Miró painted this, he was poor and hungry. Perhaps that's why the main figure, the Harlequin, has a hole in his guitar-shaped stomach. He looks sad and still in this happy, playful scene. Miró said that hunger made him hallucinate, or see things that weren't really there.

WHO WAS MIRÓ?

Joan Miró was born in Spain in 1893. On a trip to Paris, France, in the 1920s, he became interested in an art style called Surrealism. He was fascinated by people's imaginations, especially children's, and became famous for his colorful paintings and sculptures that seem to come from a make-believe world.

You can paint right over squiggly lines like this one—the waxy crayon will show through.

3 Color in your picture with water-based paint.

Miró made sculptures, too. Try creating some **mad monsters** out of modeling clay!

Let your imagination go wild with these

CRAZY CREATURES

1 On a piece of thick white paper, draw some shapes in black crayon. Don't think about it too much—just draw!

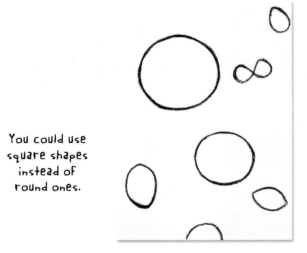

You could use square shapes instead of round ones.

2 Now start adding lines, swirls, and other shapes. Turn your page into a circus of crazy creatures!

Let some lines go right to the edge of the page.

TOTEM POLES

Wayne Alfred and Beau Dick 1991
and Ellen Neel 1955 (near left)

It's hard to imagine that these colorful carvings began life as whole cedar trees! Totem poles show the skill of traditional artists from the northwest coast of North America.

Tall stories

It can take a year to carve a totem pole! The idea is to tell a story, perhaps about an event, a legend, or people in a particular family. Each pole is a stack of characters that have special meaning in the local culture. Many animals and birds are believed to have special powers or to bring different kinds of luck.

The green-faced figure on the far left is Red Cedar Bark Man. In traditional tales, he survived a great flood and gave people the first canoe. You can see him holding a patterned boat, with the legendary Quolus bird spreading its wings above him. Quolus is the younger brother of Thunderbird, who tops the pole on the near left.

TOTEM TRADITION

Native Americans have carved totem poles for hundreds of years, but because wood rots, the oldest examples have not survived. These two were made by modern-day artists from the Kwakwaka'wakw tribe of British Columbia, Canada. You can tell they are modern because of the bright paint colors.

Make your own totem pole out of a cardboard tube and paper!

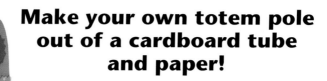

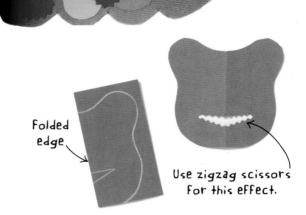

Folded edge

Use zigzag scissors for this effect.

2 Cut out some simple animal shapes. To make them symmetrical, cut them from a folded piece of paper.

Cut slits in the top of the tube to slot the wings in.

4 Wrap your finished design around the tube and tape it on the back. For a final touch, you could make some colorful cardboard wings.

CRAFTY TOTEM

The Thunderbird brings thunder with his flapping wings and lightning with a flash of his eyes! Below him is Sea-Bear and a killer whale, then a man with a frog. Lower down we see the yellow-nosed Bakwas—"wild man of the woods"—and Dzunukwa, a child-eating giantess. They are all characters from Kwakwaka'wakw legend.

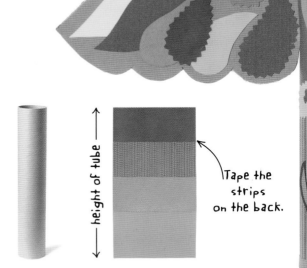

← height of tube →

Tape the strips on the back.

1 Cut some paper so that it's the right size to wrap around your tube. You could tape several strips together, like this.

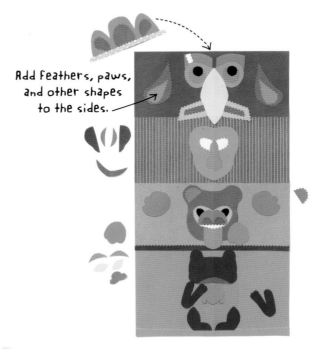

Add feathers, paws, and other shapes to the sides.

3 Glue your animals down the center of the paper. The more shapes you cut and layer, the more decorative the pole will look.

YELLOW COW

Franz Marc 1911

Have you ever seen a yellow cow with blue spots? Probably not! Franz Marc loved to paint from nature, but he didn't copy exactly what he saw.

Inside out

Marc said that he wanted to re-create animals "from the inside." He used colors to express different feelings. For him, yellow was cheerful, gentle, and female—like this cow, leaping happily across a sunny scene.

Marc's style of painting is known as Expressionism. It captures a mood rather than a realistic view of the world and makes us look at things in a different way. In fact, Marc knew very well how to paint a realistic cow. He spent long hours sketching and studying animals and even taught other artists about their shape and form.

WHO WAS MARC?

Franz Marc was born in Germany in 1880, the son of a landscape painter. He took up art at the age of 20 and was soon organizing exhibitions with other Expressionist artists. Marc was fascinated by animals. He wanted to paint the world through their eyes. Sadly, he died young, fighting in World War I.

Yellow makes a lively, happy sheep.

2 Look at the color and decide how it makes you feel. Think of that mood as you paint in the sheep's head and legs.

This green is gloomy for a grumpy sheep.

How do colors make you feel? Find out with these
MOODY SHEEP

1 Pick a paint color and squeeze some onto a palette or paper plate. Dip a sponge in the paint and use it to paint a fluffy sheep's body.

Lilac is calm for a snoozy sheep.

3 Repeat steps 1 and 2 using different colors.

What colors would you use for an **angry sheep**, a **lazy sheep**, or a **startled** one?

4 Why not make a big picture with all of your moody sheep? Take a large piece of paper or posterboard and sponge paint a colorful background. Cut out your sheep and glue them on!

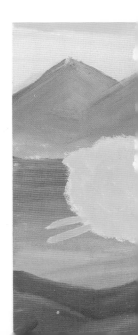

DRAGON DISH

Chinese artist 1600–1635

A snake's body, an eagle's claws, the scales of a fish . . . you can see several animals in a Chinese dragon!

These dragons are painted on a porcelain dish, surrounded by decorative swirls.

Curious creatures

Artists can have fun with dragons because they're imaginary—no one really knows what they look like! In Chinese mythology, they are often friendly, unlike the fire-breathing dragons of Europe. They are rulers of water and the weather and symbols of power and good luck.

These three dragons have lizardlike head frills and wriggling bodies that twist around the dish. Their four claws show that they are ordinary dragons—five claws would mean they belonged to an emperor. The round shapes that the dragons are chasing are magical flaming pearls. Everything is painted in a single color—cobalt blue. The artist used a fine brush for the detail and then filled in the outlines. In some parts, the color is layered to give a darker effect.

HOW WAS IT MADE?

This type of ceramic painting is called "underglaze blue." The blue design is painted onto dried white porcelain and then coated with a clear protective glaze. Afterward it is baked, or fired, at a high temperature. This hardens the porcelain and sets the glaze.

3 Experiment with different brushstrokes before adding detail to your dragon.

Use the tip of a fine brush for delicate lines.

A flick of a brush gives scaly shapes like this.

Try a sideways dab of the brush . . .

. . . and long, sideways strokes.

4 Decorate your dragon with scales and fins. Add swirling patterns around it.

You could add a thin coat of glitter paint to make your dragon gleam!

Transform a paper plate with your own

DISHY DRAGON

1 Sketch your dragon in pencil first. Draw the head and then a long, snakelike body and tail. Add four legs with clawed feet.

When this dish was made, artists didn't have paints like ours. Instead they used pigments—solid cakes of color that they ground into powder and mixed with liquid. This blue comes from a substance called cobalt. It has been used in Chinese pottery for more than 1,000 years.

2 Use a fine brush and thick paint to cover the outline in blue. Then color it in with a wide brush and watery paint.

You can layer more color to make some areas darker.

PORTRAIT OF MAURICE

Andy Warhol 1976

Andy Warhol was known for his pictures of rich and famous people—but he happily made portraits of their pets, too! This dachshund belonged to the art collector Gabrielle Keiller.

Dazzling dog

Maurice the dachshund wasn't actually blue, pink, and red! Warhol liked experimenting with bold, attention-grabbing colors—they reminded him of advertisements and modern life. He took photographs of Maurice and then worked on them back in his studio. To make this screen print, he pushed ink through a type of stencil on a silk screen.

Warhol once wrote, "I never met a pet I didn't like"—and, in fact, he had two dachshunds of his own. You can see his love of animals in this portrait of Maurice, who looks straight at us with appealing eyes.

WHO WAS WARHOL?

Andy Warhol was born in the United States in 1928. His talent for art showed from a young age, and he loved movies, photography, and cartoons. He became famous for his Pop Art inspired by advertising images and glamorous stars. Archie, one of his dachshunds, was often photographed by his side!

3 When the paint is dry, lift the stencil and move it slightly down and to one side. Sponge red paint unevenly over it and then leave it to dry.

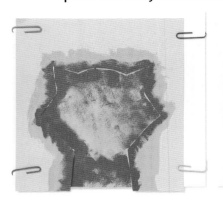
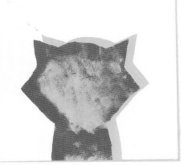

4 Now lay Stencil 2 on top of the picture and sponge blue paint over the holes. Leave it to dry, and then remove the stencil. Cut out the animal and stick it onto a colored background.

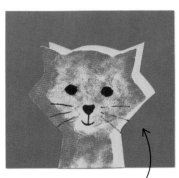

You can print whiskers by dipping the edge of a strip of card stock in paint.

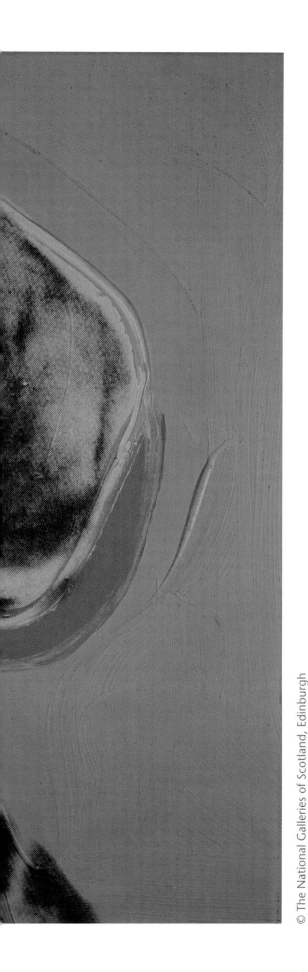

COLORFUL CATS

Warhol's silk-screen method was complicated, but **you can get a similar effect with a simple stencil.**

1 On a piece of card stock, draw the outline of an animal and carefully cut it out. You'll end up with two stencils like these.

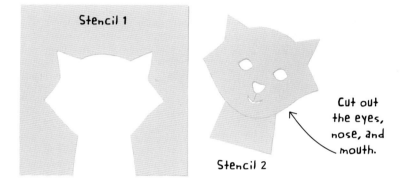

Stencil 1

Cut out the eyes, nose, and mouth.

Stencil 2

2 Lay Stencil 1 on a piece of thick paper and attach it with paper clips. Sponge yellow paint all over it.

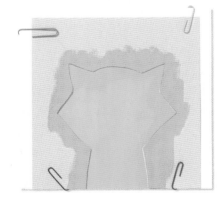

Warhol often repeated his prints in different colors. **Try making a set like this!**